W9-BVJ-286

THE SEA

A Photographic Voyage

With Writings by John Kennedy, Thor Heyerdahl, Sir Francis Chichester, Anne Morrow Lindbergh, Jacques Cousteau, Rachel Carson and Others

Selected by Dee Danner Barwick

♛ HALLMARK CROWN EDITIONS

ARNULFO L. OLIVEIRA MEMORIAL LIBRARY
1825 MAY STREET
BROWNSVILLE, TEXAS 78520

"The Great Birds" by Kenneth Patchen, *When We Were Here Together.* Copyright 1952 by Kenneth Patchen and © 1957 by New Directions Publishing Corporation. Reprinted by permission of New Directions Publishing Corporation. "Young Sea" from *Chicago Poems* by Carl Sandburg. Copyright 1916 by Holt, Rinehart and Winston, Inc. Copyright 1944 by Carl Sandburg. Reprinted by permission of Holt, Rinehart and Winston, Inc. Excerpt from *Peter Freuchen's Book of the Seven Seas* by Peter Freuchen. Copyright © 1957 by Simon & Schuster, Inc. Reprinted by permission of Simon & Schuster, Inc. "The Same Storms" reprinted by permission of Coward-McCann, Inc., from *Gipsy Moth Circles the World* by Sir Francis Chichester. Copyright © 1967 by Sir Francis Chichester. "Sea Love" from *The Sense of Wonder* by Rachel Carson, Harper & Row, 1965. Reprinted by permission of Harper & Row, Publishers, Inc. "The Spool and the Lighthouse" from *Collected Poems* by Winfield Townley Scott. Copyright © 1941, 1959 by Winfield Townley Scott. Reprinted by permission of The Macmillan Company. "Sea Fever" from *Poems* by John Masefield. Copyright 1912 by The Macmillan Company, renewed 1940 by John Masefield. Reprinted with permission of The Macmillan Company. Genesis 1:9-10 from the *Revised Standard Version Bible,* reprinted with permission from the National Council of the Churches of Christ. Excerpt from *Gift From the Sea,* copyright © 1955 by Anne Morrow Lindbergh, reprinted by permission of Random House, Inc. "La Mar" reprinted by permission of Charles Scribner's Sons from *The Old Man and the Sea,* pages 32-33, by Ernest Hemingway. Copyright 1952 Ernest Hemingway. Excerpt from *Kon-Tiki* by Thor Heyerdahl. Copyright 1950 by Thor Heyerdahl. Published in the United States by Rand McNally & Company and the rest of the world by George Allen & Unwin Ltd. Reprinted by their permissions. Excerpt from *The Living Sea* by Jacques-Yves Cousteau with James Dugan. Copyright © 1963 by Harper & Row, Publishers. Reprinted by permission of Harper & Row, Publishers. Excerpt by Arthur Rimbaud from *An Anthology of French Poetry,* edited by Angel Flores. Copyright 1958 by Angel Flores and reprinted with her permission. "The Fringe of the Sea" by A. L. Hendriks. Reprinted by permission from *The Christian Science Monitor.* © 1970 The Christian Science Publishing Society. All rights reserved. "Ships in Harbor" by David Morton. Reprinted by permission of Martha Rutan. "The Tide at Long Point" (Copyright © 1956 May Swenson) which first appeared in *The New Yorker,* is reprinted by permission of Charles Scribner's Sons from *To Mix With Time* by May Swenson. Excerpt from "Say That He Loved Old Ships" from *Bright Harbor* by Daniel Whitehead Hicky. Copyright 1932, © 1960 by Daniel Whitehead Hicky. Reprinted by permission of Holt, Rinehart and Winston, Inc. Excerpt reprinted from "Along a Beach" from *The History of the World as Pictures,* by Nancy Sullivan. Copyright 1965 by Nancy Sullivan. Used by permission of the publisher, University of Missouri Press, Columbia, Missouri. "Souvenirs" by Terry & Renny Russell in *On The Loose,* copyright © 1967 by the Sierra Club and reprinted with their permission. "The Ever Constant Sea" Copyright © 1967 by Rod McKuen and Anita Kerr. Reprinted from *Listen to the Warm,* by Rod McKuen by permission of Random House, Inc.

Copyright © 1971 by Hallmark Cards, Inc., Kansas City, Missouri.
All Rights Reserved. Printed in the United States of America.
Library of Congress Catalog Card Number: 74-155786.
Standard Book Number: 87529-189-9.

THE SEA

The breaking of a wave cannot explain the whole sea.

VLADIMIR NABOKOV

AND GOD SAID,

"Let the waters under the heavens

be gathered together into one place, and

let the dry land appear." And it was so.

God called the dry land Earth, and the waters

that were gathered together he called Seas.

And God saw that it was good.

GENESIS 1:9-10 (RSVB)

THE FRINGE OF THE SEA

We do not like to awaken
far from the fringe of the sea,
we who live upon small islands.
We like to rise up early,
quick in the agile mornings
and walk out only little distances
to look upon the water,
to know it is swaying near to us
with songs, and tides, and endless
  boatways,
and undulate patterns, and moods.

We want to be able to saunter
  beside it
slowpaced in bronzing sunlight,
barearmed, barefoot, bareheaded,
and to stoop down by the shallows
sifting the random water
between assaying fingers
like farmers do with soil,
and to think of turquoise mackerel
turning with consummate grace,
sleek, and decorous,
and elegant in high blue
  chambers.

We want to be able to walk out
  into it,
to work in it,
dive and swim and play in it,
to row and sail and pilot
over its sandless highways,
and to hear
its calls and murmurs wherever
  we may be.

All who have lived upon small
  islands
want to sleep and awaken
close to the fringe of the sea.

A. L. HENDRIKS

FROM WHENCE WE CAME: I really don't know why it is that all of us are so committed to the sea, except I think it's because in addition to the fact that the sea changes, and the light changes, and ships change, it's because we all came from the sea. And it is an interesting biological fact that all of us have in our veins the exact same percentage of salt in our blood that exists in the ocean, and, therefore, we have salt in our blood, in our sweat, in our tears. We are tied to the ocean. And when we go back to the sea—whether it is to sail or to watch it—we are going back from whence we came.

JOHN F. KENNEDY

The greatest resource of the ocean
is not material but the boundless spring
of inspiration and well-being we gain from her.

JACQUES COUSTEAU

from ALONG A BEACH

The shore beheld us and we ducked.
Into a deep blue cabin. Watching
The beach from the pleasure boat
It looked a vaudeville. Arms were waving.
The scene was happy as a cracker:
Shrieks and the hoopla of summer.
The life guard blew his whistle.

We are bulging on the beach.
Each man, himself inside his trunks;
Each woman, buttocks, breast, and belly:
The essence of the sea that sways—
Pendulous, full up.

All the children, like marvelous dolls,
Are driving us crazy.
They dig deep holes in the sand
That fill with water.
    Even the castles level.

The fishermen come all dressed to the sea.
Their boots and hats suggest
    some inland meeting
As they sponge over the beach to the
    fanciful rocks....

NANCY SULLIVAN

Do you not find a strange analogy
to something in yourself?
For as this appalling ocean
surrounds the verdant land,
so in the soul of man there lies
our insular Tahiti,
full of peace and joy....

HERMAN MELVILLE

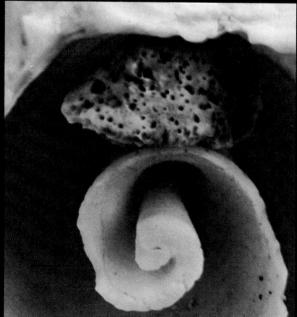
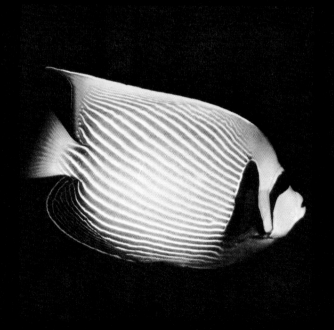

The sea is God's thoughts spread out. GEORGE DOUGLAS

IT TOOK MANKIND ALMOST THE whole of human history to discover how vast the Pacific is—almost to the end of the eighteenth century geographers just couldn't believe that there is so much sea, and insisted on "balancing" the globe with a wholly imaginary Great Southern Continent…. No one can sail in these seas without thinking of the great seamen in their often cranky sixteenth, seventeenth and eighteenth century ships who slowly displaced legend with geographical fact, and added to man's knowledge of the world—Magellan, Drake, Anson, Fernandez de Quiros, Dampier, Bougainville and, above all, Cook. We shared the same ocean and the same storms….

SIR FRANCIS CHICHESTER

YOUNG SEA

The sea is never still.
It pounds on the shore
Restless as a young heart,
Hunting.

The sea speaks
And only the stormy hearts
Know what it says:
It is the face
       of a rough mother speaking.

The sea is young.
One storm cleans all the hoar
And loosens the age of it.
I hear it laughing, reckless.

They love the sea,
Men who ride on it
And know they will die
Under the salt of it.

Let only the young come,
  Says the sea.
Let them kiss my face
  And hear me.

I am the last word
  And I tell
Where storms and stars come from.

CARL SANDBURG

[THE OLD MAN] ALWAYS THOUGHT OF THE SEA AS *LA MAR* WHICH IS what people call her in Spanish when they love her. Sometimes those who love her say bad things of her but they are always said as though she were a woman. Some of the younger fishermen…spoke of her as *el mar* which is masculine. They spoke of her as a contestant or a place or even an enemy. But the old man always thought of her as feminine and as something that gave or withheld great favors, and if she did wild or wicked things it was because she could not help them. The moon affects her as it does a woman….

ERNEST HEMINGWAY
The Old Man and the Sea

I have discovered it.
What? Eternity.
It is the sea
Matched with the sun.

ARTHUR RIMBAUD

THE EVER-CONSTANT SEA

Once upon a time
loving set me free.
Free as any bird who ever heard
the wind blow in the trees.

After love had gone
I had merely me
and my only friend
the ever-constant sea.

We've been through it all
my old friend and me.
Summertime and fall have shown us all
the world there is to see.

So, if I love again
if love is good to me
I'll share it with my friend
the ever-constant sea.

ROD MCKUEN

HOW WONDERFUL ARE ISLANDS!
Islands in space...ringed about by miles
of water, linked by no bridges, no cables,
no telephones. An island from the world
and the world's life.

People, too, become like islands in such
an atmosphere, self-contained, whole
and serene, standing back in reverence
before the miracle of another individual.

ANNE MORROW LINDBERGH

THE GREAT BIRDS

A gentle wind blows in from the water.
Along the banks great birds are walking.
It is morning....
  Oh! what a lovely morning! Slowly the
great birds rise into the soft golden
air above the village....A strand of your
hair touches my cheek.
  How much better for the world had
nothing else ever happened in it.

KENNETH PATCHEN

THE SEA GYPSY

I am fevered with the sunset,
I am fretful with the bay,
For the wander-thirst is on me
And my soul is in Cathay.

There's a schooner in the offing,
With her topsails shot with fire,
And my heart has gone aboard her
For the Islands of Desire.

I must forth again to-morrow!
With the sunset I must be
Hull down on the trail of rapture
In the wonder of the sea.

RICHARD HOVEY

WHEN GALES WHIP THE TREES AND RATTLE OUR WINDOWS OR SNOW piles up outside so that no one wants to go for a walk, landlubbers snug in warm rooms are likely to tell each other how sorry they feel for all the poor sailors on a night like this. But they feel, too, a little wistful envy of the men who brave cold and storms upon the restless water. Then on a fine day the sight of foreign seamen or of tall ships from far away or of an exotic bit of merchandise from halfway round the world or even of an oddly shaped scrap of driftwood cast up on the beach gives any of us a pang of jealousy of the men who move about over the sea viewing the wonders of the deep. And it must be confessed that these wonders lose nothing in the seamen's telling of them.

The stories which these fellows bring to us are the stuff our dreams are made of. We may not believe the tellers of the salty tales for a minute, but in our secret minds we live them. We all are great heroes in our dreams. We drift endlessly in hot, dead calms while all on board but us are in despair. We baffle the most violent storms, conquer the bravest fighters, foil the most blood-thirsty pirates, bring home the richest cargoes from the most amazing voyages, wrestle with monsters, dive for sunken gold, see the strangest sights. Then, in the end, science takes over from imagination—and behold, there are even greater wonders than we dreamed.   PETER FREUCHEN

He that will learn to pray,
let him go to sea.

GEORGE HERBERT

Say that he loved old ships; write nothing more
   Upon the stone above his resting place;
And they who read will know he loved the roar
   Of breakers white as starlight, shadow lace
Of purple twilights on a quiet sea....

DANIEL WHITEHEAD HICKY

SHIPS IN HARBOR

I have not known a quieter thing than ships,
   Nor any dreamers steeped in dream as these;
For all that they have known disastrous seas,
And winds that left their sails in flagging strips,
Nothing disturbs them now, no stormy grips
   That once had hurt their sides, no crash or swell;
   Nor can the fretful harbor quite dispel
The quiet that they learned on lonely trips.

They have no part in all your noisy noons;
   They are become as dreams of ships that go
   Back to the secret waters that they know,
Each as she will, to unforgot lagoons,
   Where nothing moves except the ghostly spars
That mark the patient watches on the stars.

DAVID MORTON

Always going. The beam of time spins
A halo, and what was dark on earth
Is dark; but what was bright recedes
Always going....

WINFIELD TOWNLEY SCOTT

SEA FEVER

I must go down to the seas again,
    to the lonely sea and the sky,
And all I ask is a tall ship
    and a star to steer her by;
And the wheel's kick and the wind's song
    and the white sail's shaking,
And a gray mist on the sea's face,
    and a gray dawn breaking.

I must go down to the seas again,
    for the call of the running tide
Is a wild call and a clear call
    that may not be denied;
And all I ask is a windy day
    with the white clouds flying,
And the flung spray and the blown spume,
    and the seagulls crying.

I must go down to the seas again,
    to the vagrant gipsy life,
To the gull's way and the whale's way
    where the wind's like a whetted knife;
And all I ask is a merry yarn
    from a laughing fellow-rover,
And quiet sleep and a sweet dream
    when the long trick's over.

JOHN MASEFIELD

SOUVENIRS

We leave: part of ourselves.
We take: sand in our cuffs, rocks, shells,
     moss, acorns, driftwood, cones, pebbles,
     flowers,
Photographs.

But is the picture a tenth of the thing?
A hundredth?
Is it anything without the smell and salt
     breeze and the yellow warmth when
     the fog lifts?

Oh! but I got all that, too.
It is exposed forever on the sensitive
     emulsion sheet
Of my mind.

TERRY AND RENNY RUSSELL

ARNULFO L. OLIVEIRA MEMORIAL LIBRARY
1825 MAY STREET
BROWNSVILLE, TEXAS 78520

Doris G. Barker: *Page 43(L).*

Richard Beattie, ALPHA: *Pages 4, 5.*

Color Library International: *Pages 28, 29.*

Jim Cozad: *Page 36.*

Peggo Cromer: *Page 32.*

Dr. E. R. Degginger: *Front Endpaper, Pages 7,*
   18(UL, UR, LR), 19, 31, 39(B), 43(R), 46(R), 48.

Phoebe Dunn: *Pages 34, 35, 47, 49(T), 53(L), 57, 60*

Richard Fanolio: *Page 18(LL).*

Harv Gariety: *Page 11(L).*

Grant M. Haist: *Page 53(T).*

Dennis Hallinan, ALPHA: *Page 12.*

David Jenkins: *Page 33.*

Jack Jonathan: *Pages 8(B), 14, 16, 17, 22, 59.*

Joe Klemovich: *Pages 44, 55.*

John Kohout, Root Resources: *Page 15(B).*

Charles Mueller: *Page 27.*

David Muench: *Title Page, Pages 3, 25, 61.*

National Aeronautics and Space Administration: *Page 23*

Larry Nicholson: *Page 49(B).*

H. Armstrong Roberts: *Pages 20, 21, 51.*

Fran Rogers: *Pages 8(T), 10, 15(T), 42, 46(L)*

David Strout: *Pages 37, 38, 39(T), 40(B).*

Myron Wang: *Back Endpaper.*

Dr. John C. Weaver: *Pages 26(L, R), 40(T).*

Jack Zehrt: *Pages 13, 45.*

Set in Linofilm Palatino.

Designed by William M. Gilmore.

PN
6084
.035
B3

APR 2 9 1997

MAY 1 8 1997

LEARNING RESOURCE CENTER
1825 May St. Ft. Brown
Brownsville, Texas 78520

Brownsville Public
Cameron County
Pan American University Brownsville
Texas Southmost College

City-College Library
1825 May Street
Brownsville, TX 78520